THE CALL OF GOD

PASTOR (MRS.) SHADE OLUKOYA

THE CALL OF GOD

© 2005 PASTOR (MRS.) SHADE OLUKOYA

ISBN: 978 - 38233 - 4 - 5

1st Printing – August 2005 AD

Published by:

The Battle Cry Christian Ministries

11, Gbeto Street, Off Iyana Church Bus Stop, Iwaya Road, Iwaya, Yaba, P.O. Box 12272, Ikeja, Lagos.

Website: www.battlecrying.com

Email: battlecrying@representative.com

Phone: 0803-304-4239, 0803-332-2376, 0803-306-0073, 0802-303-3938, 0803-309-8246, 0803-315-7249, 0803-305-4142.

FOREIGN CORRESPONDENCES
UNITED STATES
Phone: 404 – 454 – 3358

GHANA
Phone: 24236113

All scripture quotations are from the King James version of the Bible.
Cover illustration: Pastor (Mrs.) Shade Olukoya

TABLE OF CONTENTS

FOREWARD

The call of God comes in various ways. Your destiny in life is determined by God's call. When we talk about the call of God, it does not necessarily mean that you are called to be a pastor or a deliverance minister. Generally speaking, the call of God centres on becoming whom and what God destines you to be in life. You cannot achieve the fulfillment of your destiny in every department of your life without discovering, understanding and working out the divine blueprint for your life.

The problem of destiny diversion, stems from total ignorance concerning the divine destiny of the individual. Herein lies the greatest problem of man. Many people are blind to what God has destined them to become. Others who have a little knowledge in this area have been sentenced to aimless wandering by the powers of their father's house. Against this backdrop, the author has addressed a subject which will result into the resurrection of buried destinies.

I commend this book to all those who want to live their lives to the maximum and achieve the purpose for which God has sent them into the world. My prayer for you is that, God will continue to awaken the giant in you until your life will echo the words of the scriptures.

2 Tim 4:7-8: I have fought a good fight, I have finished my course, I have kept the faith: Henceforth there is laid up for me a crown of righteousness, which the Lord, the righteous judge, shall give me at that day: and not to me only, but unto all them also that love his appearing.

Dr. D.K. Olukoya
15th July, 2005

CHAPTER ONE

THE CALL OF GOD

The call of God is a message for everyone to consider. From the beginning, God has been in the business of calling men and women to carry out His assignment in the world. Everything God created has its place in the over all work of God. In the book of Genesis, the word of God says God created two kinds of light. The greater light to rule the day and the season of the night is for the light of the moon and the stars. You have a place in the work and the same service of God. The call of God is to fix you where exactly God has made you to belong.

Gen 1:14-18: And God said, Let there be lights in the firmament of the heaven to divide the day from the night; and let them be for signs, and for seasons, and for days, and years: And let them be for lights in the firmament of the heaven to give light upon the earth: and it was so. And God made two great lights; the greater light to rule the day, and the lesser light to rule the night: he made the stars also. And God set them in the firmament of the heaven to give light upon the earth, And to rule over the day and over the night, and to divide the light from the darkness: and God saw that it was good.

IGNORANCE IS A HINDRANCE

You cannot fulfill a call you don't know about. If you are looking for a job, you have to keep your ears on the ground for vacancy advertisement in the media. Job owners often advertise available vacancies in their organizations. They specify the kind of labour they need. It could be skilled or unskilled labour. They also specify certificate and experience qualifications necessary to fill available positions. Most of them generally give a time limit within which any interested applicant should apply. If you do not know that there is a vacancy suitable for you, you cannot fill it. Ignorance of available vacancy suitable for your talents, personality, experiences and qualifications will keep you away from the job you should be doing.

This is what happens in spiritual things. Your ignorance of the call of God will render you useless when and where you should be useful. As advertisement has a time frame you must know and fulfill the call of God. As the best qualified candidate for a vacancy may continue to roam the streets without a job, because of his ignorance of where his services are needed, a child of God with great spiritual potentials may continue to waste away, because of ignorance of the call of God upon his or her life. You should begin to pray seriously to know the call of God upon your life.

IT IS YOUR DESTINY

The call of God is your destiny. It should be taken seriously, because that is what you are in the world to do. Many people have gross misconception in this area. They try to avoid the call of God, because of their selfish interest and carnal ambition. Ignorance is keeping them away from destiny fulfillment. The call of God is what will enable you to fulfill the purpose of God for your life. It is your destiny. Whatever you are doing besides what God has called you to do is a direct enemy of your destiny irrespective of your success in that area. If you want to fulfill your destiny and receive the call of God upon your life and prepare your heart to fulfill it.

THE NECESSITY OF A CALL

It is necessary to be called into an assignment before you start doing it. You can not impress God by doing what He did not ask you to do. As important as preaching to save souls is, it cannot be done without being called into it. A sinner must first obey the call to the new birth experience before he can run with the vision of saving others.

Rom 10:13-15: For whosoever shall call upon the name of the Lord shall be saved. How then shall they call on him in whom they have not believed? and how shall they believe in him of whom they have not heard? and how shall they hear without a preacher? And how shall they preach, except they be sent? as it is written, How beautiful are the feet of them that preach the gospel of peace, and bring glad tidings of good things

The great question preceding the salvation of souls is

that how can preachers preach God's message, except they are sent to do so? This question hits directly on the necessity of a call. An assignment may be urgent. It may be very important to be done. Without being called and sent to do it, you cannot do it to please God.

The question you should begin to ask yourself is who sent you the work you are doing right now? You can decode to usurp the position of God in your life or do whatever you feel should be done for God. The question is who sent you? A preacher may have the full gospel message in his heart and there may be multitudes before him who need the message, however God must give the order before he starts preaching.

It is rebellion against the order of God to engage yourself in an assignment which God had not called you to do. Who sent you into your present area of career? Who you sent your into present area of career? Who sent you into the department you are in the Church? Who sent you to the location you are now? Who sent you into the business you are doing? Who sent you to the organization where you are working? Ask yourself these questions and discover the call of God upon your life.

The call of God is often considered with narrow-mindedness to conclude it is all about ministry work in the kingdom. The call into an area of service or ministry in the Church is just a part of the over all call of God. The call of God covers all areas of life because He uses every means to carry out His great works among men.

If God did not call you into the marriage in which you are now your family will lack the glory and beauty of a godly home God needs to save other families. If God did not call you into your present career and profession, you cannot be a vessel to propagate His glory and power among your colleagues. Daniel, Shedrach, Meschack and Abednego found themselves in Babylon according to divine order. It was, therefore, easy for God to use their academic careers to propagate His glory and power in the ancient Babylonian empire.

Dan 1:3-4: And the king spake unto Ashpenaz the master of his eunuchs, that he should bring certain of the children of Israel, and of the king's seed, and of the princes; Children in whom was no blemish, but well favoured, and skilful in all wisdom, and cunning in knowledge, and understanding science, and such as had ability in them to stand in the king's palace, and whom they might teach the learning and the tongue of the Chaldeans.

Dan 1:17-20: As for these four children, God gave them knowledge and skill in all learning and wisdom: and Daniel had understanding in all visions and dreams. Now at the end of the days that the king had said he should bring them in, then the prince of the eunuchs brought them in before

Nebuchadnezzar. And the king communed with them; and among them all was found none like Daniel, Hananiah, Mishael, and Azariah: therefore stood they before the king. And in all matters of wisdom and understanding, that the king inquired of them, he found them ten times better than all the magicians and astrologers that were in all his realm.

The beginning of God's demonstration of power in Babylon was through the careers of the four Hebrew children. They excelled throughout Babylon and the king took note of their outstanding performances. Daniel, Shedrach, Meschack and Abednego did not work miracles, but God used them to manifest the miracle of academic excellence among, the chaldeans. God used them because they found themselves in the right place doing the right thing. If they had stayed back among the remnant in Israel, it would have hindered God from using their careers to His glory.

The problem with you is not that you belong to an unpopular department of the Church. You problem is not that your profession is not an high demand in the market. The real problem with you is not that you certificate on vocational training is not longer demanded oin the labour market as before. The issue with your marriage is not really that modern men and woman are difficult to manage in marriage. The problem with you is not necessarily your location. The real problem is whether God sent you into what you are doing or not. The primary problem is whether God called you to where you are now. The call of God is such a necessity that you cannot do anything without ascertaining it.

GLORIOUS BEAUTY

The glorious beauty of a life is the fulfillment of God's call. Those who recognize the call of God and are sent into His assignment are described as having beautiful feet. Go back to the book of Romans which we read before and look at verse fifteen.

Rom 10:15: And how shall they preach, except they be sent? as it is written, How beautiful are the feet of them that preach the gospel of peace, and bring glad tidings of good things!

Responding to the call of God is what makes a beautiful life. Fulfilling the call of God is what makes a glorious life. Everybody admires beauty. This is the secret behind the appreciation, honour and love men and women enjoy as they fulfill the call of God for their lives. God makes everything beautiful in its own time. The feet of Paul was beautiful as he went about preaching the gospel. This is your own time. Your feet can be beautiful as you walk in the path of fulfilling the call of God. Men and women, everywhere, will want to emulate you and stamp their feet on your beautiful footprints.

THE WORK OF GOD AND YOU

You are important to fulfilling God's assignment in the world. When God has a work to do, He looks for men and women to use. Angels have their irreplaceable roles in the work of God. However, there are areas of service that are exclusively reserved for men and women to run. The works of men and the ministry of angels do not contrast. Rather, they complement each other.

Heb 1:14: Are they not all ministering spirits, sent forth to minister for them who shall be heirs of salvation?

God Himself made the place of man undoubtedly clear. There was a time He planned to visit the children of Israel with revival, what He did was to look for a man to run the divine errand.

Ezek 22:30: And I sought for a man among them, that should make up the hedge, and stand in the gap before me for the land, that I should not destroy it: but I found none.

Whether a man or a woman, you belong to the central force of the work of God. There are many things God

Page (15)

will not do until He finds the right man or woman to use. You can begin to imagine to what extent you have hindered the work of God by not accepting His call. The warning of Nineveh against impending doom was followed by national repentance. Divine wrath was averted from both old and young because the whole country repented at the preaching of only one man. Imagine what eternal doom and damnation the disobedience of one man would have brought upon a while country.

Until you begin to walk in the call of God, you wouldn't know what you have been hindering God to do. Most ministers of God in their ministries could not have imagined what proportion of works God could do through them at the beginning of their calling. In your mind, picture a congregation of over twenty thousand worshippers in an area of five million population. Imagine that the pastor of that congregation choses to disobey the call of God. What would be the lot of the congregation?

God takes the issue of His call upon men and woman seriously because of what is attacked to it. He has not stopped calling people, because of the significance of the call. Those who refuse and disobey the call of God are judged on the balance of what God should have achieved through them. What would have made God to send Jonah into the belly of a fish for a fervent prayer of repentance with fasting for three days? He wanted him to have a feel of the agony of perdition the people of Nineveh would suffer if he refused to preach to them. Jonah called the belly of the fish hell.

Jonah 2:1-2: Then Jonah prayed unto the LORD his God out of the fish's belly, And said, I cried by reason of mine affliction unto the LORD, and he heard me; out of the belly of hell cried I, and thou heardest my voice.

The confession of Jonah illustrates the agony those who disobey the call of God go through. As Jonah prayed from the hell of the fish's belly, disobedient people have a hell of experiences. Talk about their finances, it is a hell of experience from the point of disobeying the call of God. Talk about their marriage and family life, it is hell on earth. Talk about their career, it is the fire of hell. Talk about their security and protection, they suffer a hell of attacks. Talk about their health, they experience a hell of mysterious sicknesses. Find out the cause of the hell of experiences you have been going through. It may be linked with your refusal to accept the call of God.

CHAPTER TWO

THE SPECIAL CALL

There are people whom God significantly used for outstanding purposes. Their call occupied a place in the programme of God which not everybody could occupy. These men and women were called into specific assignments and deep relationship and fellowship with God so that they become a pattern for many generations to come. Such people are forerunners of God's new moves, bearers of God's newest revelations to His people, fighters of the modern battle of God, foundations for a strong faith structure to come and special partners in the topmost agenda and business of the invisible God.

You cannot just wake up one day and compare yourself with them. Their examples are there to inspire and guide you. But they generally don't belong to a class anybody can boast to fall into in a day or two. Let us look at some of them below.

ABRAHAM

Abraham was not just a man of faith, he was a symbol of faith and faithfulness to every believer in Christ. Nobody before Abraham ever had his kind of faith in the way God called him into fellowship and obedience. His story came after the flood. Since there was no written record of the faith of his predecessors like Noah, Enoch and others, he stood in an isolated world of faith life. Abraham started a career in faithful relationship with God without reference materials about the men that lived before him. God called him, he just obeyed.

Gen 12:1: Now the LORD had said unto Abram, Get thee out of thy country, and from thy kindred, and from thy father's house, unto a land that I will shew thee:

Gen 12:4-5: So Abram departed, as the LORD had spoken unto him; and Lot went with him: and Abram was seventy and five years old when he departed out of Haran. And Abram took Sarai his wife, and Lot his brother's son, and all their substance that they had gathered, and the souls that they had gotten in Haran; and they went forth to go into the land of Canaan; and into the land of Canaan they came.

The faith of Abraham has remained a classic of all times. There was never a record of any man so called by God. In the plan of God to start a new relationship with mankind, Abraham was the starting point. His foundation and history with God was to become a pattern for all who would walk with God by faith. Today, we are encouraged by his faith and faithfulness of others because of the advantage of the complete scriptures, Christian literatures and tapes, ministers of the gospel, fellow believers and a full measure of the Holy Ghost measure around us. Abraham did not have these, yet he became a pattern of the life of faith.

ENOCH

Enoch was a symbol of walking with God. The emphasis of the revelation of God about Enoch was his walk with God. Look at how the Bible introduces his relationship with God.

Gen 5:22-24: And Enoch walked with God after he begat Methuselah three hundred years, and begat sons and daughters: And all the days of Enoch were three hundred sixty and five years: And Enoch walked with God: and he was not; for God took him.

In only three verse of the scriptures, the Holy Ghost reiterates the relationship of Enoch's practical life with God in two verses. In verses twenty two and twenty four, we read "And Enoch walked with God" twice.

There was something about this man's walk with God. No man ever walked with God that way since the creation of Adam and Eve. God called Enoch into a life that became a pattern of walking with God.

Enoch walked with God despite having sons and daughters. This is where you will know that the man was outstanding. Many single brothers and sisters are not walking with God in the pattern of Enoch. Many married people who are yet to have children are far from the pattern of Enoch's walk with God. Let me not even talk about those whose complaints are about their wayward children. Enoch walked with God and heaven decided that he was not fit to die.

Men might have been making advances to his daughters before they married. Ladies might have been visiting his sons before they married. Nothing in the environment of Enoch could hinder his walk with God. His family and vocational life was not a barrier at all. In the midst of what surrounded him, God concluded that he so much pleased Him to escape death among men. Enoch walked with God and because a pattern of walking with God for all believers.

JACOB

Jacob was a symbol of warfare. Here was a man who had the promise God did not give his twin brother. He represents a man or woman whom God distinguishes among his or her contemporaries by divine promises. But Jacob lived a life that towers above that of his contemporaries.

Having a grasp of the promises that went forth in his favour before birth, he set himself to achieve them by his own methods. He exercised all the skills in him. Realising he was naturally endowed with cleverness, he found strength in his skills and began to draw various master plans to obtain the promises of God.

The more he planned and hatched his plans, the more the promises evaded him, until he found the importance of Peniel as a turning point in his life. At Peniel, the struggles, strength, skills, talents, abilities and cleverness of a man met divine resistance. The man was broken and the divine promises came to fulfillment.

Gen 32:24-31: And Jacob was left alone; and there wrestled a man with him until the breaking of the day. And when he saw that he prevailed not against him, he touched the hollow of his thigh; and the hollow of Jacob's thigh was out of joint, as he wrestled with him. And he said, Let me go, for the day breaketh. And he said, I will not let thee go, except thou bless me. And he said unto him, What is thy name? And he said, Jacob. And he said, Thy name shall be called no more Jacob, but Israel: for as a prince hast thou power with God and with men, and hast prevailed. And Jacob asked him, and said, Tell me, I pray thee, thy name. And he said, Wherefore is it that thou dost ask after my name? And he blessed him there. And Jacob called the name of the place Peniel: for I have seen God face to face, and my life is preserved. And as he passed over Penuel the sun rose upon him, and he halted upon his thigh.

God brought Jacob into the centre of His dealings with men as a pattern for those who would not naturally give up for God. He became a lesson for us to learn that only God can fulfill His promises not our carnal schemes and skills.

For a while, Jacob's eyes were taken away from the promises of God to look upon God who gave them. He was taught the bitter lesson of keeping his grasp away from the promises, and shifting focus on God. He left God's promises. He held unto God who gave them. And what has eluded him for years became fulfilled in his life. He used the weapon of spiritual warfare. If you prevail against satan and demons, you are a very good soldier. But when you prevail with God in prayers, you become a prince.

DEBORAH

Deborah was a symbol of strength in a weaker vessel. She stands for courage from the most unexpected vessel. Deborah was a symbol of heroism in the affairs of the Almighty God. Her example convinces us that a woman can become a heroin in the affairs of God. A woman can become a champion in the battles of the Lord. A woman can play a supportive role to a man, without which the ministry of the man cannot be fulfilled. Deborah stands to affirm the fact that there are affairs of God's kingdom that are not complete without the ministry of women.

Judg 5:6-7: In the days of Shamgar the son of Anath, in the days of Jael, the highways were unoccupied, and the travellers walked through byways. The inhabitants of the villages ceased, they ceased in Israel, until that I Deborah arose, that I arose a mother in Israel.

Deborah was the first female commander of the army of the Lord. General Barak would not go to war without Deborah. Imagine the glory and power of this woman in the midst of God's children. She emerged a leader when there was none to lead the flock of the Lord. She emerged a judge when there was none to hear the conflicts of God's children. She emerged a prophetess when the voice of God was scarce in the land. You cannot quantify what God can achieve through you as a woman. God can even begin something entirely new with you.

God can make your ministry an inevitable complement to that of a man or your husband. God is still looking for Deborah. There are battles God still wants to fight using a modern day Deborah as an instrument. God is seeking to recruit Deborahs who would put the enemies to flight. God is looking for Deborahs who chase the captains of God's enemies to fall at the feet of a fellow woman. Will God find you a Deborah in your generation? Consider the call of God upon your life.

Judg 5:24-27: Blessed above women shall Jael the wife of Heber the Kenite be, blessed shall she be above women in the tent. He asked water, and she gave him milk; she brought forth butter in a lordly dish. She put her hand to the nail, and her right hand to the workmen's hammer; and with the hammer she smote Sisera, she smote off his head, when she had pierced and stricken through his temples. At her feet he bowed, he fell, he lay down: at her feet he bowed, he fell: where he bowed, there he fell down dead.

RUTH

Ruth was a symbol of unconditional love. She was a pattern of patience and perseverance. As in the cases of others in her category, Ruth became the first woman to take and hold on to her decision to the end. Orpah took a similar decision, but her compromise on the way stand to show the firmness of Ruth's decision. Do you think it is a light matter to stand where others fall? Do you think it is a joke to remain firm in your decision when your closest partners crumble by the way side?

Ruth stood against all persuasion to rescind on her decision. She moved on in the strength of unconditional love.

Ruth 1:8-14: And Naomi said unto her two daughters in law, Go, return each to her mother's house: the LORD deal kindly with you, as ye have dealt with the dead, and with me. The LORD grant you that ye may find rest, each of you in the house of her husband. Then she kissed them; and they lifted up their voice, and wept. And they said unto her, Surely we will return with thee unto thy people. And Naomi said, Turn again, my daughters: why will ye go with me? are there yet any more sons in my womb, that they may be your husbands? Turn again, my daughters, go your way; for I am too old to have an husband. If I should say, I have hope, if I should have an husband also to night, and should also bear sons; Would ye tarry for them till they were grown? would ye stay for them from having husbands? nay, my daughters; for it grieveth me much for your sakes that the hand of the LORD is gone out against me. And they lifted up their voice, and wept again: and Orpah kissed her mother in law; but Ruth clave unto her.

Ruth had the secret many Christians don't have today. Her secret was unconditional love. Those who love Christ on the condition that He heals, delivers, prospers, protects, etc don't go too far with Him. Orpah's love was conditioned upon getting a husband to marry. When it dawned on her that it was not likely to be so, she turned her back on the road to serving the true and the living God.

Not many Christians can stand like Ruth. Orpah was her partner in marriage and fellowship. Many people are backsliding today because of their backslidden friends. Many are turning away from Christ because their friends no longer come; you will agree with me that this woman was a pattern of love and persistence. Her determination to follow her decision through was too strong for the strongest opposition to defeat.

Ruth 1:15-18: And she said, Behold, thy sister in law is gone back unto her people, and unto her gods: return thou after thy sister in law. And Ruth said, Intreat me not to leave thee, or to return from following after thee: for whither thou goest, I will go; and where thou lodgest, I will lodge: thy people shall be my people, and thy God my God: Where thou diest, will I die, and there will I be buried: the LORD do so to me, and more also, if ought but death part thee and me. When she saw that she was stedfastly minded to go with her, then she left speaking unto her.

Do you know what it means for a woman's determination and love to silence the strongest voice of opposition? Do you know what it means for a woman to be shown the picture of an uncertain future and yet she decided to go for it? Do you know that Naomi was the only witness who could tell Ruth about the God of Israel and the children of Israel? From her words, Naomi, the only true witnesses, discouraged her. She spoke as though there was no hope for her. Naomi, the only witness, spoke as if she was wasting time going with her to Israel. All these did not change Ruth's decision.

My sister, how would you feel if Jesus the true witness from heaven told you there is no heaven? How would you feel if Jesus the healer said there is no healing for you?

How would you feel if Jesus the deliverer said there is no deliverance for you. I can continue this question and apply it to many different areas of your life.

This is why you will understand that God dealt with in an outstanding manner. She was a pattern. Her determination was supernaturally sustained by God. Her decision was supernaturally backed up by the invisible palm of God's hand. She did not live to regret her decision, love, persistence and determination. She got a husband to marry and became the great grandmother of the Lord Jesus Christ.

CHAPTER THREE

THE SCHOOL OF CHRISTIAN SERVICE

Moses was a symbol and pattern of deliverance. The scope of deliverance he represents goes beyond the affairs of an individual. Many people are happy to see God use them to set just one person free. Like the disciples of Jesus, they would go places to celebrate their victory over one demon they cast out from an individual. Moses stood on a ground so high in the programme of God that he is likened to Christ in many respects. He was called to deliver a whole country from the bondage of another country.

Ex 3:7-10: And the LORD said, I have surely seen the affliction of my people which are in Egypt, and have heard their cry by reason of their taskmasters; for I know their sorrows; And I am come down to deliver them out of the hand of the Egyptians, and to bring them up out of that land unto a good land and a large, unto a land flowing with milk and honey; unto the place of the Canaanites, and the Hittites, and the Amorites, and the Perizzites, and the Hivites, and the Jebusites. Now therefore, behold, the cry of the children of Israel is come unto me: and I have also seen the oppression wherewith the Egyptians oppress them. Come now therefore, and I will send thee unto Pharaoh, that thou mayest bring forth my people the children of Israel out of Egypt.

As a pattern and symbol of deliverance, Moses had the army of Egypt to face. The wrath of Pharaoh was waiting for him. The powers of darkness operating in Egypt were all against him. The bondage of Israel in Egypt had a spiritual dimension. They were in bondage physically because they were in bondage spiritually. Moses was called

PASTOR (MRS.) SHADE OLUKOYA

to face the magicians, sorcerers and demonic personalities of Egypt.

It is spiritual pride to think you can just wake from sleep and perform Moses' kind of miracles that led to the deliverance of the children of Israel. If you ever had to cast out a demon that proved stubborn before finally bowing out, you would understand the intensity of spiritual opposition Moses met in Egypt.

God put this man in a strategic place in his programme to teach us that there is no spiritual opposition He cannot use us to break. Moses example teaches us to know that God can defeat the strongest gathering of the powers of darkness. What made the difference in his life was his response to the call of God. It would have been impossible to deliver Israel from the Egyptian bondage if God had not sent Moses to the assignment from experience, he knew, it was humanly impossible to liberate Israel, because the first and only attempt he made led to his flight from Egypt.

Ex 2:11-15: And it came to pass in those days, when Moses was grown, that he went out unto his brethren, and looked on their burdens: and he spied an Egyptian smiting an Hebrew, one of his brethren. And he looked this way and that way, and when he saw that there was no man, he slew the Egyptian, and hid him in the sand. And when he went out the second day, behold, two men of the Hebrews strove together: and he said to him that did the wrong, Wherefore smitest thou thy fellow? And he said, Who made thee a prince and a judge over us? intendest thou to kill me, as thou killedst the Egyptian? And Moses feared, and said, Surely this thing is known. Now when Pharaoh heard this thing, he sought to slay Moses. But Moses fled from the face of Pharaoh, and dwelt in the land of Midian: and he sat down by a well.

The human attempt he made to deliver only one Israelite from the hands of just one Egyptian put his name on the death row of Pharaoh. Death was very certain for him, because he took up an assignment God did not send him that time. This is the mystery about the call of God. You will fail in any venture into which God has not sent you. You will fail in any assignment God has not committed to your hands. Moses fled for safety from a field of ministry the Lord did not approve for him at that time.

Defeat in ministry has a message of its own. It is either you have failed to do everything necessary to succeed or you are in a corner were God has not positioned you. This recurrent defeat you always experience may mean more than not praying enough. Even Elijah could not pray down the power, glory and fire of God or Mount Carmel, until he was sure God wanted him to do so. When he began to pray, he reminded God that he was doing everything according to divine instructions.

1 Kings 18:36-39: And it came to pass at the time of the offering of the evening sacrifice, that Elijah the prophet came near, and said, LORD God of Abraham, Isaac, and of Israel, let it be known this day that thou art God in Israel, and that I am thy servant, and that I have done all these things at thy word. Hear me, O LORD, hear me, that this people may know that thou art the LORD God, and that thou hast turned their heart back again. Then the fire of the LORD fell, and consumed the burnt sacrifice, and the wood, and the stones, and the dust, and licked up the water that was in the trench. And when all the people saw it, they fell on their faces: and they said, The LORD, he is the God; the LORD, he is the God.

FOOD FOR THOUGHT

Can you pray in your marriage and challenge God that you came into contract at His word? Can you pray and command God to bless the works of your hands that you started at His word? Can you pray as a pastor, woman leader and church leader that the glory and power of God should fall from heaven, because you are in your present location at His word? This is the all important question you must answer before going on in life. There is nothing that can replace or substitute the call of God in the life of a man.

If God called you into what you are doing now, the defeat, opposition, satanic threats, mountains and problems are all there as an opportunity for God to prove His power and glory on your behalf. If God did not call you, the negative signs you are seeing are enough to help you retrace your steps. There is no substitute to the call of God.

What happened when Moses went back to Egypt? He faced Pharaoh and declared the counsel of God. Remember, he did not even went to see Pharaoh face to face before he ran away from Egypt. He knew Pharaoh wanted to kill him and he fled. But with the backing of God's call, he was now the one looking for Pharaoh. He was the one now interrogating Pharaoh. The call of God gives the power, courage and boldness to confront the enemies you once ran away from.

Ex 5:1: And afterward Moses and Aaron went in, and told Pharaoh, Thus saith the LORD God of Israel, Let my people go, that they may hold a feast unto me in the wilderness.

ISAIAH
Isaiah was a symbol of the messianic prophet. Although he did not live in the era of grace brought by Jesus, he saw so much about the time of Christ that his writings are full of references to Him.

The call of God upon this man brought him into an experience meant for another age. He saw Jesus long before He was born. He saw His glory, power and everlasting kingdom. Isaiah saw the righteousness that would characterize the reign of Christ. He saw the grace of God in the days when the law ruled.

Only the call of God could give a man that advantage in the things of the spirit. Isaiah was like a primary school pupil who was privileged to see the curriculum of university works. It was a rare privilege. His book is full of the gospel of Christ at a time Christ was yet to be born.

Isaiah's example convinces us that the call of God can position us for advantages for which our age, time, dispensation, etc are not qualified. What I said is not impossible at all. It is not outside scriptural harmony. I give you two instances from previous records to the account of Isaiah. Enoch was the first man to be raptured. Elijah was the second man to go to heaven alive. These men did not belong to the time of the rapture at all. But God gave them a fore-taste of what was to come in the church age.

There are deep experiences with God that no average believer can just experience except by the call of God. There are mysteries of God that no average minister can be let into except according to the call and purpose of God. Isaiah enjoyed grace while under the Law. If he were to live today under grace, only God can tell what he would be enjoying.

JOB

Job was a pattern and symbol of victory in suffering. Nobody has ever come close to his experience in the experience of calamities. At the time of Job, it was said that no righteous man ever had a similar experience. He was so outstanding in his troubles that when God decided to visit him, he was given outstanding double portion of everything he ever lost.

Job 42:12: So the LORD blessed the latter end of Job more than his beginning: for he had fourteen thousand sheep, and six thousand camels, and a thousand yoke of oxen, and a thousand she asses.

You cannot have Job's exact experience. But he has been set forth as a pattern and consolation for everyone going through in explicable calamities, troubles, problems, storms and experiences. The Holy Ghost, in Jesus, refers us to the patience of Job after all that befell him. In his case, Job was a man called to suffer terrible trouble as a pattern and symbol for those who would go through any hard time in life. His patience and latter end are documented so that by them; we may have hope and courage.

CHAPTER FOUR

WHEN GOD CALLS YOU

You cannot inherit the call of God. Before you accept to work as a minister of God, you must be sure of the call of God upon your life. Anointing can be imparted, gifts can be transferred. But you cannot inherit the call of God. Even if your father or mother was a minister of God, you cannot inherit his or her call. That your parents are ministers of God today does not mean that the call of God will automatically fall on you. God called Samuel and his son could not inherit the call.

1 Samuel 8:1-5: And it came to pass, when Samuel was old, that he made his sons judges over Israel. ow the name of his firstborn was Joel; and the name of his second, Abiah: they were judges in Beer-sheba. And his sons walked not in his ways, but turned aside after lucre, and took bribes, and perverted judgment. Then all the elders of Israel gathered themselves together, and came to Samuel unto Ramah, And said unto him, Behold, thou art old, and thy sons walk not in thy ways: now make us a king to judge us like all the nations.

God deals with individuals and groups of people. When it comes to the call of God, He separates issues and makes His mind clear. Where God wants to bring two or three persons together as partners in a particular assignment, God must call them individually. Everyone in group work or team ministry should have a personal testimony and experience of divine call. After God spoke to Moses about the assignment in Egypt; He also spoke to Aaron about it.

Exodus 4:27-30: And the LORD said to Aaron, Go into the wilderness to meet Moses. And he went, and met him in the mount of God, and kissed him. And Moses told Aaron all the words of the LORD who had sent him, and all the signs which he had commanded him. And Moses and Aaron went and gathered together all the elders of the children of Israel: And Aaron spake all the words which the LORD had spoken unto Moses, and did the signs in the sight of the people.

Don't cram yourself into the group of pastors, leaders, prayer warriors, choir members etc. because of the glory and power of God among them. God must call you to do so, if not, you will become the Jonah that will cause their ship to sink if you are not quickly thrown out. This is where the trouble is with modern ministers of God. They don't have their personal testimonies but whatever testimonies others have, whose group they belong, no matter how many people are in a group, God calls and deals with them as individuals. Before God spoke to Aaron, He had told Moses about him as his partner in ministry.

Exodus 4:14-16: And the anger of the LORD was kindled against Moses, and he said, Is not Aaron the Levite thy brother? I know that he can speak well. And also, behold, he cometh forth to meet thee: and when he seeth thee, he will be glad in his heart. And thou shalt speak unto him, and put words in his mouth: and I will be with thy mouth, and with his mouth, and will teach you what ye shall do. And he shall be thy spokesman unto the people: and he shall be, even he shall be to thee instead of a mouth, and thou shalt be to him instead of God.

God made it clear to Moses that Aaron was coming to play a supportive role in his ministry. God made it clear to Aaron himself what assignment he needed to carry out with Moses. Let us draw a lesson here. If God clearly spoke to two people individually and independently for partnership in ministry work, how much more where we have a group of more than two ministers? Let me ask you again, in the group where you belong, did God call you into it? What you are doing presently? Did God approve it for you?

AGE IS NOT A BARRIER

Age is not a barrier to the call of God. At your present age, you belong somewhere in the programme and call of God. Unlike in secular services where age is either a barrier or a disadvantage, the call of God spreads across all age categories. What I am, therefore, saying in essence is that at your present age, you are neither too old nor too young to know about the call of God and obey it.

I have talked much about Moses. His life was divided into three phases. For the first forty years, he was learning the wisdom and education of the Egyptians. The next forty years of his life, he was a shepherd man in the house of Jethro, his father-in-law. At eighty God called him to deliver Israel from the bondage of Egypt. He fulfilled his ministry for the third forty years of his life, winding up everything at the age of one hundred and twenty years.

Jesus knew His mission before He came to the world. At the age of twelve, He already had enough knowledge and wisdom to confound the lawyers and Pharisees around Him. Nevertheless, Jesus did not begin His full public ministry until He was thirty years of age. He ran His ministry for only three and half years and the whole world is full of books and commentaries about Him.

Thirty is an age in the life of a man or woman where much tirelessness and energy is displayed. At that age when His contemporaries were driven by the zest to conquer the world through secular knowledge and method, God put Jesus in the full pursuit of the heavenly vision. Don't make a mistake by thinking the call of God can only come to you when you are much older and retiring in life. The call of God can interrupt your youthfulness, ambition, energy etc at an early age and veer your off into the mission of God.

Abraham was called at seventy-five years of age. He was obviously an old man at that age. But God called him into a life of faith and obedience that became a permanent reference point in the believer's relationship with God.

This man of exemplary faith, faithfulness and obedience was called at his old age. It is wrong notion to think that God cannot use old people in the Church. It is absolutely incorrect to think that old people in the Church don't have anything to offer.

Age is no banner to the works and workings of God. Abraham and Sarah, his wife, were a couple who no longer had the energies of their youth, but they had the kind of faith that entered into the record of God forever. Don't write yourself off because of your age. I agree you may be old and fragile, you are not too old for God to use. Moreover, you are not as old as the Ancient of Days Himself.

Old men and women may not be physically strong to do activities that require manual labour in the Church. They can be exemplary in living a faith challenging life. They can be giants in prayers and intercession. They can be reservoirs of the deep mysteries of God because of their experiences coupled with divine inspiration. I, therefore, appeal to you that even in the prime of your life. God can call and use you to His own glory.

Jeremiah was called of God. He was less than twenty years when God called him. If a sample of our youth's activities is taken by statistics across the country, the result will be morally ridiculous and generally wasteful. The devil has hijacked many lives between fifteen and twenty age brackets. During his time, Jeremiah belonged to this age category and the call of God came upon his life. Old people want God to give them more time to settle everything about their children and grandchildren. Young people want God to allow them to marry and achieve success before considering His call. God does not look at human conveniences and before calling men to His service.

BACKGROUND IS NOT A BARRIER

It is a lazy attitude to attribute failure in life to the circumstances surrounding our birth and background. There is never a problem without a solution. You couldn't decide your kind of background before you were born, but you can change everything you don't desire in your background through prayer.

Background is not a barrier to the call of God. From all fields of human endeavours, God has been calling men. Your background is used by God to prepare you for the call of God later in life. David was a shepherded boy, he was called to lead the flock of God. Moses was a shepherd, he to was called to lead the sheep of God. Amos was also a shepherd; he was called into the office of a prophet to declare the counsel of God.

Peter was a fisherman, he was called to become a fisher of men. Matthew was a tax collector he was called to preach the gospel that will enable men to pay their souls to God as a tax for living in the world he created. Paul was a lawyer and a Pharisee, he was called into true defense of the gospel of Christ. Luke was a physician, he was called into the business of saving lives for eternity. Your vocational and professional background is not a barrier to the call of God form reaching you.

CHAPTER FIVE

THE QUALITIES OF GOD'S CALL

The call of God has some qualities that make it different from other callings.

1. **Powerful:** The call of God is powerful. When it comes, you will know, because it comes powerfully. Whatever the method God chooses to use to communicate His call to you, you will notice that the call is powerful. It is because of this quality about it that men cannot resist or successfully throw it aside.

2. **Supernatural:** The supernatural experiences or manifestations than accompany the call of God help to distinguish it from other callings. Moses saw a burning bush that was not consumed, and then a voice spoke with him. Gideon saw an angel that spoke with him. There is something supernatural about the call of God.

3. **Unmistakable:** You cannot mistake the call of God. You may be immature to handle it or recognize it at first; you will find it unmistakable in the end. When Go called Samuel, though he mistakenly went to Eli, it was unmistakable that he heard a voice call his name.

4. **Unforgettable:** The call of God is unforgettable. All throughout the ministry of Paul, he never stopped

talking about his supernatural encounter on the road to Damascus, because the experience was unforgettable in his life. Those who claim to have had the call of God but forget it in pursuit of business are doubtful if God ever called them.

IMPACTS OF DIVINE CALL

Divine call is not an experience without impact. You are the first person to felt the impact of the call of God upon your life before other people do. What are the impacts of the divine call.

1. **You Will Know It:** If you have a divine call, you will know it. God makes it so clear that you won't be in the dark about it. Before other witnesses confirm it to you, you will have a personal knowledge of it that God has called you.

2. **You Will Feel The Anointing:** There is an anointing that accompanies divine call that you will feel upon your life as an evidence. The anointing makes everything about you extra-ordinary.

3. **Blue Print:** God gives the blue print of His plans to those He calls. Moses was taken to the mountain-top and was given the blue print of the tabernacle. He was

strictly informed to make sure he built everything according to the heavenly pattern he saw on the mountain.

4. **Clear Vision:** Without a clear vision, there will be nothing to pursue. It is the clear vision that God gives you that enables you to run in the direction of your assignment.

5. **Divine Equipment:** There are gifts God releases to back you up and help you fulfill your call. The gifts are divine equipment and tools with which you are to work. As an employer provides materials to enable your carry out your duties, so the Lord equips those He calls with gifts.

TWO KINDS OF CALL

The men and women God called in the Bible can be categorized into two.

1. **General Call:** There are assignments God calls His children into without exception. This kind of call is called universal call. It is an area of service where everybody can participate. Under the general call of God, we have the following

a. **Personal Evangelism:** Personal evangelism is a ministry for every child of God. As soon as you are born again, you don't have to wait until God makes you an evangelist or apostle before you start preaching the gospel. Jesus told His disciples:

Mark 16:15: And he said unto them, Go ye into all the world, and preach the gospel to every creature.

The only qualification for this ministry is to be a disciple. A disciple is a believer in Christ and His follower. Many Christians do no know that personal evangelism is a springboard for the higher calling of God. You are doing a great job if you take personal evangelism seriously. The disciples recorded great success on their fields of assignment as they embarked on intensive personal evangelism. There is personal evangelism for everyone to do and there is specific office of an evangelist.

Luke 10:17: And the seventy returned again with joy, saying, Lord, even the devils are subject unto us through thy name.

b. **Intercession:** Praying and intercessory ministry is also under the general call of God. There is a level of praying every child of God must be involved in. When the Bible says we should pray without ceasing, it is not an assignment only for pastors. It is a call of God to every believer Paul desired prayer support from the Church of Jesus Christ and he knew everybody in that assembly was not a minister of the gospel in the higher sense of the word. But there is another level of praying and depth of intercession into which God specifically calls some people. They have an anointing to operate and function at higher efficiency than an average praying believer. Generally, every believer is admonished to:

1 Thess 5:17: *Pray without ceasing.*

c. **Deliverance:** Maybe you are surprised to know that deliverance ministry is for every child of God. You cannot separate deliverance from personal evangelism. Under the general call to go and preach the gospel, there is also the general commission to cast out devils, which is deliverance ministration.

Matthew 10:18: Heal the sick, cleanse the lepers, raise the dead, cast out devils: freely ye have received, freely give.

There is a level of deliverance ministration every believer should be able to handle. In the Mountain of Fire and Miracles Ministries we teach that personal deliverance is possible. Again, Jesus has given the mandate and He is supporting the work. The disciples generally went everywhere preaching and the Lord confirmed their messages with signs following. The signs include the miracles of deliverances. In this area again, there are people whom God specially and specifically anoints to carry out much deeper and thorough deliverance works. These are deliverance ministers. There level of anointing is different and they achieve more results with ease.

d. **Healing:** The promise of God for every believer is to lay hands on the sick for their recovery. You don't have to be a healing evangelist before you can do this. There is a level of healing ministry that is part of personal evangelism. And there is another level of healing ministry into which God specially calls some people.

Luke 9:2: And he sent them to preach the kingdom of God, and to heal the sick.

e. **Singing:** in the epistle of Peter, the holy spirit says we are redeemed to show for the praises of our God. In that sense, every believer is expected to operate at a general level of singing ministry. Paul also wrote and told a whole church that they should admonish themselves, singing psalms and spiritual songs. The singing ministry is a wonderful ministry into which God specially calls men and women, but there is the general class of it for every believer in Christ. Paul was not a chorister or choir master, but he sang along with Silas and there was an earthquake.

Col 3:16: Let the word of Christ dwell in you richly in all wisdom; teaching and admonishing one another in psalms and hymns and spiritual songs, singing with grace in your hearts to the Lord.

1 Peter 2:9: But ye are a chosen generation, a royal priesthood, an holy nation, a peculiar people; that ye should shew forth the praises of him who hath called you out of darkness into his marvellous light:

f. **Good Works:** The Bible describes us as God's workmanship in Christ, created for good works. Good works include helping people, giving, showing kindness and hospitality, showing mercy and doing good generally. When some Christians want to defend their stingy spirits, they claim not to have the gift of giving. But when Jesus commands us to "give" He was not referring to those with the calling of an apostle alone or those with the gifts of giving. Good works is another area of general ministry for every child of god to run.

But God gives some people outstanding grace in these areas so that hey excels above others in the same exercise.

Eph 2:10: For we are his workmanship, created in Christ Jesus unto good works, which God hath before ordained that we should walk in them.

If you think you don't have the call of God upon your life because you are not a pulpit pastor, travelling evangelist, prophet, apostle and so on, it is because you are ignorant of God's general call into these various ministries above. You are not supposed to be idle in the house of God. There is so much to do that labourers are even few. This book is an eye opener for you to discover the call of God upon your life.

2. **Special Call:** Apart from the general call of God, there is individual, specific and special call of God. Everybody does not belong here. You really have to pray and be sure of your stand when it comes to this kind of call. The services in this category are more tasking, difficult, demanding and much harder. There is no grace to function under a special call if you have not been called specially. The five-fold ministry comes under this kind of call.

Eph 4:11: And he gave some, apostles; and some, prophets; and some, evangelists; and some, pastors and teachers;

The people with special call are chosen by God's sovereign wisdom and power. They are not elected by Church committee or popular opinion. Some of them might not even be seeking God before the divine call interrupts their lives. Paul was a good example. On the road to Damascus, he was not seeking God, neither was he fasting nor praying. But God met him suddenly and commissioned him. A similar thing happened to apostle Joseph Ayo Babalola. He was just busy doing his roadwork when the call of God came upon him.

CHAPTER SIX

DIVINE SUPPORT FOR THE CALL

People who are specially called and anointed by God have some characteristics.

1. **They Are Very Scarce:** They are not always common. If you put the population of born again children of God together and select those with special call of God upon their lives, you will be amazed to see how few they are. They are not too many in every generation. Jesus has many disciples, only twelve of them were apostles during His earthly ministry.

Luke 6:13: And when it was day, he called unto him his disciples: and of them he chose twelve, whom also he named apostles;

2. **They Are Very Powerful:** Manifestation and demonstration of supernatural powers is a basic characteristic of men and women with a special call of God. The measure of power that flows in their lives and ministries is far more than what can be found, sometimes in the collective gathering of other children of God.

3. **They Are Effective:** People with special call are effective. Philip was appointed among those to take care of food matters in the early Church. But God gave him a special call into the office of an evangelist.

He went down to Samaria and single handedly turned the city upside down for Jesus. He was effective.

Acts 8:5: Then Philip went down to the city of Samaria, and preached Christ unto them.

4. **They Don't Live For Long:** Sadly, some of these people don't live for long according to the divine purpose of God. John the Baptist had a special call as the only forerunner of Jesus Christ of all men ever born of a woman. But he lived for a short time. Jesus Himself was killed at the end of His three and half years of ministry. He was a little above thirty-three years when He wound up His ministry and life. Apostle Joseph Ayo Babalola, our unforgettable pentecostal father did not live for long too. God chooses and removes them as He pleases.

PITFALLS OF SPECIAL CALL

You may have the special call of God upon your life. I congratulate you. It will, therefore, do you much good to consider the pitfalls associated with special callings and avoid them.

1. **Pride:** The greatest danger hunting men and women with special call is pride. Except God really works on

them to produce incorruptible humility, pride is a problem the devil uses to pull them down.

Prov 16:18: Pride goeth before destruction, and an haughty spirit before a fall.

2. **Conceit:** This is another danger nearer people with special call than others. The tendency to have an overblown opinion of themselves is all to high. In the world of today, some men and women with special call have wrecked their chances with God through self-conceit. Some woke up to declare they are what God did not say they are. Titles like "last witness:, "last prophet", "last apostle" etc only show the self delusion of those who adopted them.

3. **Carelessness:** With so much spiritual power, it is easy to be careless and carefree. As the grace and anointing of God increase upon your life and you perceive God's special hand upon you, watch against carelessness. Don't be too big to attend Bible studies, prayer meetings and Church services.

Heb 10:25: Not forsaking the assembling of ourselves together, as the manner of some is; but exhorting one another: and so much the more, as ye see the day approaching.

God calls people in His sovereignty. Some people run to Jesus because of satanic attacks. The Lord delivers and commissions them to His service. The third category of people whom God calls are those who come to the Lord because of their love for Him. They come and receive His call upon their lives.

CHARACTERISTICS OF TRUE DIVINE CALL

1. **Spiritual Conviction:** a true call of God is not about feeling in the head or body. It is spiritual conviction. In the heart of your heart, you will be convinced that God has called you. Those who say, "I think ;;;", "I feel .." or "They say …" God has called them don't know what they are talking about yet.

2. **Personal Experience:** The call of God is an individual personal experience. It is not collective or by committee recommendation.

3. **Signs And Wonders:** There are signs that accompany everyone that is called of God. Even in the class of general call, we are told;

Mark 16:17: And these signs shall follow them that believe; In my name shall they cast out devils; they shall speak with new tongues;

4. **Clear Divine Voice:** God devises a way he speaks with those He calls. Improve on His method of communication with you, which could be through dreams, visions, prophecies etc.

5. **Special Assignment:** The call of God has a specific assignment to carry out. Divine call is not vague. Moses was told to go and deliver Israel from bondage. The Lord told Samuel to anoint David king over His people. Paul was called an apostle to the gentiles. In MFM, we are called into warfare prayer, deliverances, revival of apostolic signs, holiness within and without, training warriors, separation from the world and showing people the way.

6. **Obstacles Will Bow:** With a divine call upon your life, obstacles will bow before you. Mountain could not stand before Zerubabel because of the call of God upon his life.

Zech 4:7: Who art thou, O great mountain? before Zerubbabel thou shalt become a plain: and he shall bring forth the headstone thereof with shoutings, crying, Grace, grace unto it.

DIVINE SUPPORT FOR DIVINE CALL
God supports those He calls for His work. The God

who called Daniel closed the mouth of the lions against him and brought him out of the their den. He replaced him with his enemies and the same lions tore them. God called David and enabled him to defeat Goliath. God called Moses and parted the Red Sea before him. The Lord will give you personal healing to make your ministry outstanding. Don't be afraid to accept and fulfill the call of God. He is there to support you. He is the awesome God.

WHAT YOU MUST DO

Your responsibility in fulfilling your divine call is to do all things whole-heartedly. Find your place in the body of Christ. Take the following steps.

1. **Be Obedient:** God requires full and total obedience from everyone He calls.

2. **Be Faithful:** The testimony of God about Moses is that he was faithful in all the house of God concerning everything God told him to do. Be faithful. It is required in stewardship to be found faithful.

3. **Be Committed:** Give your whole life and time to fulfilling your call.

4. **Be Focused:** Don't lose the target of your ministerial assignment. Success or failure can derail you from your focus. Don't be carried away.

5. **Be Prayerful:** The wheels of ministerial responsibilities are run on prayers. Jesus started with prayer and ended with prayer. You can never succeed in ministry without prayers.

6. **Be Holy:** Whatever you calling and office, remember you are serving a holy God. So be holy at all times. Without holiness, you cannot see God. Even if you win the whole world for Christ, you have not achieved anything.

Be sure God called you because there is danger in running an errand which God did not send you. It is dangerous to be fulfilling a call you are not given. Nobody can just take it upon himself to become ambassador for his country without government's approval or appointment. And no ambassador can just choose to relocate to another country without the consent of the government of his country. It is dangerous to go when God has not said, "go".

WHAT THE DIVINE CALL ENTAILS

The call of God is a call into fifteen things.

1. Call to decision
2. Call to discipleship
3. Call to deliverance
4. Call to humility
5. Call to childlikeness
6. Call to sincerity
7. Call to fellowship
8. Call to excellence
9. Call to greatness
10. Call to integrity
11. Call to prayer
12. Call to the ministry of helps
13. Call to fulfillment
14. Call to faithfulness
15. Call to witnessing

THE DON'TS OF TRUE DIVINE CALL

There are things which those with the call of God must avoid.

1. They don't exhibit disloyalty
2. They don't bite the fingers that fed them.
3. They don't scatter, they gather

4. They don't lie to cover up
5. They don't worry about tomorrow
6. They don't steal their master's money
7. They don't undermine authority
8. They don't play Church politics
9. They don't pull others down in order to rise
10. They don't get involved in anything that can harm the Church.

WHO WILL GO?

God is looking for men and women to do His work. As the Church of Jesus Christ grows, so the work of the Lord grows likewise. For example, in the Mountain of Fire and Miracles Ministries we need women to rise up and join the ministerial work force. Any woman who is truely called can serve the Lord in meaningful ways. Doors of opportunities are opening. We need more female pastors to pastor Churches at home and abroad. Jesus saw the magnitude of the work before He left the world.

Matt 9:27: And when Jesus departed thence, two blind men followed him, crying, and saying, Thou Son of David, have mercy on us.

The question God asked Isaiah is what He is asking you today.

Isa 6:8: Also I heard the voice of the Lord, saying, Whom shall I send, and who will go for us? Then said I, Here am I; send me.

If you really want to respond like Isaiah and whole hearted say;

"Here I am, send me"

You have to be sure you are born again. God cannot use an unconverted soul. The choice is yours. Respond to the call of God and watch Him make the difference in your life and ministry.

PRAYER POINTS

1. Oh Lord, forgive me in any way that I have let you down in Jesus name.

2. Oh Lord, send your fire into the foundation of my life and let every enemy of my calling die in the name of Jesus.

3. Oh Lord, let the spirit of rebellion in me die in the name of Jesus.

4. Oh Lord, purge me with your fire and change me to your best today in the name of Jesus.

5. Oh Lord, send your fire into the root of my life, let every enemy of success die in the name of Jesus.

6. My father, let thy fire of deliverance fall upon me in the name of Jesus

7. Oh Lord, let your fire of revival fall upon me in the name of Jesus

8. Oh Lord, let your fire touch my spirit, soul and body in the name of Jesus

Other Publications By Dr. D. K. Olukoya

1. Be Prepared
2. Breakthrough Prayers For Business Professionals
3. Brokenness
4. Born Great, But Tied Down
5. Can God Trust You?
6. Criminals In The House Of God
7. Contending For The Kingdom
8. Dealing With Satanic Exchange
9. Dealing With Local Satanic Technology
10. Dealing With Witchcraft Barbers
11. Dealing With Hidden Curses
12. Dealing With The Evil Powers Of Your Father's House
13. Dealing With Unprofitable Roots
14. Dealing With Tropical Demons
15. Deliverance: God's Medicine Bottle
16. Deliverance From The Limiting Powers
17. Deliverance By Fire
18. Deliverance From Spirit Husband And Spirit Wife
19. Deliverance Of The Conscience
20. Deliverance Of The Head .
21. Destiny Clinic
22. Disgracing Soul Hunters
23. Drawers Of Power From The Heavenlies
24. Dominion Prosperity
25. Evil Appetite
26. Facing Both Ways
27. Fasting And Prayer
28. Failure In The School Of Prayer
29. For We Wrestle ...
30. Holy Cry
31. Holy Fever
32. How To Obtain Personal Deliverance (Second Edition)

Other Publications By Dr. D. K. Olukoya

Other Publications By Dr. D. K. Olukoya

Other Publications By Dr. D. K. Olukoya

Other Publications By Pastor (Mrs.) Shade Olukoya

ALL OBTAINABLE AT:

1. 11, Gbeto Street, Off Iyana Church Bus Stop, Iwaya Road, Iwaya, Yaba,. P. O. Box. 12272, Ikaja, Lagos.
2. MFM International Bookshop, 13 Olasimbo, Street, Onike, Yaba, Lagos.
3. IPFY Music Connections Limited, 48, Opebi, Salvation Bus Stop (234-1-4719471, 234-0833056093)
4. All Mfm Church Branches Nationwide And Christian Bookstores.